WIZARDS HANDBOOK

How to make 50 magical spells

Anton and Mina Adams

BARNES
&NOBLE
BOOKS
NEW YORK

Contents

How to Use Your Wizards Handbook

Welcome to your first Wizards Handbook! We hope you enjoy the fun spells and magical ideas we have collected for you in this special, useful book.

Wizardry and magic have been a part of our lives since the early Ages. There is magic in virtually everything. In the early days, Witches and Wizards cast their spells using just simple everyday things, such as brooms, cooking pots, or cauldrons. You, too, can use just the simplest of things in your spellcasting – almost anything around you can be used in a spell.

However, certain types of spells need particular ingredients and items. If you are doing a spell for finding lost treasure, your spell ingredients may include green-colored things, such as a green-colored stone such as a piece of jade, or even a four-leaf clover.

The reason is that green is the color linked with Earth, and is used in all "Earthy" types of spells (see pages 40–59), like those for treasure, good luck, success, and getting what you want for Christmas!

Other types of spells are also available. "Air" type spells (see pages 60–79) are usually cast to help you feel confident, increase your brainpower, and get

noticed by the right people. "Fire" type spells (see pages 80–99) deal with healing and protection. A great anti-bully spell is described for you to try out! "Water" type spells (see pages 100–119) are all about feeling safe and secure, and include spells for making friends easily and helping clear unhappiness from your home.

We'll tell you all you need for these spells, and the best times to cast your special spell. We'll also give you any special instructions on how to prepare the spell for the best results.

You also get a whole page for your own notes with each spell or magical idea. We include a couple of questions on this page to help guide you, as "Apprentice Wizard," to record how you actually did the spell, and whether you were happy with the results! We have questions like:

☆ Did you get all the right ingredients and items for the spell?
☆ Did you notice anything "funny" after you did the spell?
☆ Did you find what you were looking for?

Have fun, and don't forget: only use spells with a good heart!

Wizard Tips

What are Spells?

A spell is a magical way of imagining what you want and making it happen in the real world. There are love spells, money spells, protection spells, and spells for getting virtually anything you want, ranging from birthday presents to help in becoming more confident.

How do they work? When you first think that you would like to cast a spell, you usually have a particular reason – for example, you would like to get enough money to buy a bike. Once you know what you want, you can consult a spell book such as this one, or make up your own spell to make sure that you get the bike.

A spell is powered by your intention to get something. But how do you tell the "world" that you want something? You just simply ask. A spell is a simple way of asking the "world" to give you what you need. By doing a spell, you are sending out a message, as if you were a lighthouse sending a message to a ship. The clearer you are about what you want, the quicker you will get results.

Why should you tell the "world" about your wants and needs? An ancient belief proposes that a great deal of energy that we cannot see zips around and within us, as well as around all the objects, buildings, plants, and flowers in the world, connecting us all together.

As we are all connected, by casting a spell, you are using this invisible energy to make a shift in what happens around us. Spellcasting is very useful magic. However, two major rules need to be followed: we must not hurt anyone by casting a spell, and we must only use this energy for good (see pages 18–19 for more on positive spellcasting).

Setting up Magically

To set up a space for spellcasting, you must first find a place where you will not be disturbed, and then set up a cone of protection around your space.

You can choose to use any space in which you feel safe and comfortable. This can be anywhere, either inside your home or outside in the garden. You can easily cast most of the spells in this book in your bedroom.

If you like spellcasting, it is always a good idea to use the same space to cast all your spells. The reason is that, after a while, just being in that space will put you in a good mood for spellcasting, which will help you get good results. Consider keeping a special area set up permanently for spellcasting.

To set up magically in your bedroom, or some other safe place, collect the following items:

☆ A small, low table, box, or crate (which you can turn upside down so that you can use the flat surface)
☆ A piece of dark blue fabric big enough to cover the table surface
☆ A small, white bowl filled with salt
☆ A small to medium box that fits under the table or inside the box (this is your "spell box")

Position the table under a window from which you can see the light of the Moon, and cover it with the cloth.

Place the bowl of salt on the table. Salt is a powerful protection against evil, and is an important ingredient for setting up your space for magic. Place this Handbook near the bowl of salt. If you want to discourage people from looking in your Handbook, place the bowl on top of the Handbook.

Before every spell, always collect all the ingredients and place them in your spell box. When you have collected all the ingredients and items for your spell, only then do you cast the spell.

Preparing Yourself: Feeling Wizardly

You need to do three important things before successfully casting your chosen spell.

First, have a shower or a bath, or, at the very least, wash your hands with soap and lots of water. While you do this, imagine that you are washing away all the troubles of the day, as well as all your doubts about whether you can get what you want and whether the spell will work.

Second, imagine that you are a powerful Wizard who is preparing himself for important magical work that will make a difference in the world.

Third, look at yourself in the mirror. Continue the image of yourself as a powerful Wizard with great power and great skill, preparing yourself to do some magic.

Focus on your breathing. Breathe in for a count of three, then breathe out for a count of four. Feel your chest expand and contract. Make your breath deeper, and imagine that your stomach, and not your chest, is expanding and contracting with every breath.

Imagine that you are seeing a special color swirling around you. This energy is the earth energy that we need to power our spells. Imagine that this energy has come from the earth and from the stars, and is mingling around you, waiting for you to direct it towards the purpose of your spell. Know that this energy is also keeping you safe, as it is both a powerful and caring energy.

Then, go to your special space, which has been set up for your spellcasting (see pages 10–11 about how to set up magically). Pick up the bowl of salt, and sprinkle the salt very lightly across all the openings to the room, such as the doorway and the windows.

Imagine that the energy swirling around you is expanding out to the walls of the room, and that it is filling the space with safe, protective energy within which you can work your magic. You are now ready to cast some spells!

Your Magical Tools

There are four standard magical tools that you can collect as an apprentice Wizard. Each tool links to the four elements of Earth, Air, Fire, and Water. In ancient wisdom, it is believed that these four elements and spirit make up everything in the world and the cosmos, including you!

Over the centuries, it was also believed that the combination of these four elements gave a person great power. It was commonly thought that the famous Philosopher's Stone was made from the perfect balance of each element. Once made, it was thought that the Philosopher's Stone could cure all disease as well as turn ordinary metals, such as tin, into gold.

This is why, in magical practices, the Wizard had magical tools that linked into the power of each element. For Earth, a Wizard would find an extraordinary looking rock or crystal, either as a flat, tablet shape, or as a ball. If you collect stones and rocks, find one that is your favorite stone. If it is fairly flat, draw the following symbol on it, which represents the four elements and spirit.

A feather represents the element of Air, while a wand represents the element of Fire (see page 38 about how to make your own Wizard's Wand). Air is symbolic of your intellect, while Fire is symbolic of your magical intentions or Willpower.

The element of Water is represented by a chalice or goblet, which can be used for spells to help you clear sadness and anger out of your life and to attract happiness and harmony into it.

The crystal, feather, wand, and chalice are your basic magic tools with which you can create your spells. Feel free to use these tools while casting any of the spells in this Handbook.

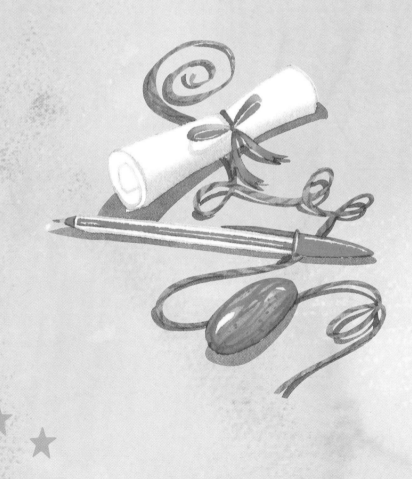

Your Magical Ingredients

The magical ingredients that you may be required to find for your spells will usually be a candle, stones or crystals, or some herbs, together with some ordinary household items, such as scissors, string, chewing gum, glue, and maybe a few sprinkles of dragonsblood!

Traditionally, dragonsblood was a fancy, bloodcurdling name for a certain plant with the botanical name of *Daemonorops draco*. It is still available, usually as a reddish powder, which can be used in spells of protection and for invisibility spells.

In the olden days, sometimes a spell needed a really hard-to-find ingredient, such as a flower that only grew at a certain time in a usually hard-to-reach place! By showing determination and no small amount of cunning,

the effort that the Wizard would put into finding that special ingredient would power the spell he was going to cast.

Also, some ancient grimoires (books of magic) had seemingly impossible instructions, such as collecting seeds from a certain plant that fell at exactly the time the sun would rise at summer solstice! This is, in fact, one of the easy ones! It was believed that the more difficult the spell, the more effective it would be, because you have to put so much thought and effort into it.

However, for modern spells, all we need to do is to imagine that our spell will be successful. Positive thinking is an important aspect of spellcasting. When you collect your ingredients, be sure to keep an image in mind of your spell being successful. For instance, imagine that you already have made it on the football team or that you have already attracted a good friend, if you are casting spells to be picked to play football for your school or if you want to find a friend.

Also, when you are collecting ingredients for your spells, make sure that they are made from natural substances – such as wooden or cardboard boxes, and fabric that is made from cotton, silk, or linen.

The Power of Doing Positive Spells

It is very important that the spells you cast are positive, and will not harm anyone or the environment. From a purely practical point of view, doing spells that harm or interfere with another person's life will attract the "Threefold Rule."

It is firmly believed by many ancient and modern Wizards and other magical workers that the energy you use to cast a spell will return to you threefold.

That is, if you are sending out positive energy, you will attract three times more positive energy. Similarly, and more worrisome, if you send out negative energy, you will get it back threefold.

So be careful what you ask for. Make sure that your spell is a positive one. Never ask for someone in particular to like you. Rather, cast a spell to attract friendship. Never ask to stop someone in particular from worrying you. Instead, cast a spell to protect you from harassment or bullying tactics.

Positive or white magic is based on honoring nature, and being respectful of the world and the people around you. The best spells come from observations of life and the world around you.

Centuries ago, just by observing the flight of birds or the movement of fish in the streams, Wizards would be able to predict the weather and could prophesize what would happen in local politics.

The most powerful of Wizards have also observed that there are strong connections between spellcraft and life. Like spellcraft, if you send out positive emotions to the people around you, you can get a lot more positive reactions back – and you will have a lot more fun!

Catching the Spirit

Celebrating Yule

What Do I Need?
A gold-colored metal or paper disc (about 3 inches/10 cm wide)
A black marker pen
A piece of mistletoe

When Do I Need to Do the Spell?
On the evening of the winter solstice (21st–23rd of December in the Northern Hemisphere; 21st–23rd of June in the Southern Hemisphere)

What Should I Do?
On the evening of winter solstice, draw the following magical symbol of the sun ☉ on the gold disc. Prop the disc against your bedroom window (or any other window) that faces the rising sun, and make a wish. You can make a wish for anything new, as Yule is the time of the birth of light and hope. Hang some mistletoe over the window and your disc, and leave it there until the sun rises the next morning. Carry your gold disc with you until your wish comes true.

Your Notes

Could you get all the ingredients? Yes ☐ No ☐

If not, list the other ingredients that you have used.

When did you do the spell? *Time*   *Day*

What Phase of the Moon is it? *New Moon* ☐ *Waxing* ☐ *Full* ☐ *Waning* ☐

What happened during the spell? What thoughts occurred to you?

Did anything odd happen after you made your wish?

Do you think your wish came true?

Empowering a Magic Carpet

What Do I Need?
A bowl with some salty water at the bottom
A rug that you can lie upon

When Do I Need to Do the Spell?
During the phase of the New Moon

What Should I Do?
Lay your rug in your bedroom or a special space where you will not be disturbed. Walk around your rug holding the bowl, sprinkling the ground very lightly with salty water. Imagine that you are cleansing the rug of all the things that make it earthbound. Now, lie on the rug and imagine that the edges are beginning to lift. Tighten your stomach muscles and imagine that you are taking off to a place of fantasy and adventure. Imagine all the sights, sounds, and smells of your new place. Bring your mind back to the rug in your bedroom, and write down what you have seen.

Your Notes

Did you do all the actions of the spell without interruption?   *Yes* ☒ *No* ☐

If you were interrupted, try the spell again later.

When did you do the spell?   *Time* 8:09 P.M. *Day* Feb. 28 2003

What Phase of the Moon is it?   *New Moon* ☒ *Waxing* ☐ *Full* ☐ *Waning* ☐

What happened during the spell? What thoughts occurred to you? I went to a castle they were baking bread and it was 1543.

Did anything odd happen after the spell? I sneezed. I don't usually sneeze.

Do you think your spell worked? Yes.

Celebrating May Day

What Do I Need?
A piece of white drawing paper
A black marker pen

When Do I Need to Do the Spell?
On the evening of the 30th of April (if you live in the Northern Hemisphere)
or the 31st of October (if you live in the Southern Hemisphere)

What Should I Do?
Draw a picture of some mountains, and a tree or shrub, with your pen on the white piece of paper. This will look like a winter scene, all white and cold. Cut out the tree or shrub shape, and prop up the picture on your bedroom window or another window of the house from which you can see a tree that is starting to turn green. The next morning, look at your picture and see the light green of the tree through your picture. Make a wish, particularly for something that you haven't been able to get yet. Springtime energy is great for getting things that have seemed impossible to get hold of during winter!

Your Notes

Could you get all the ingredients?   *Yes* ☐ *No* ☐

If not, list the other ingredients that you have used.

When did you do the spell? *Time*   *Day*

What Phase of the Moon is it?   *New Moon* ☐ *Waxing* ☐ *Full* ☐ *Waning* ☐

What happened during the spell? What thoughts occurred to you?

Did anything odd happen after the spell?

Do you think your spell worked?

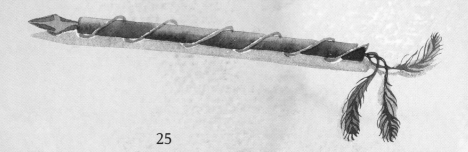

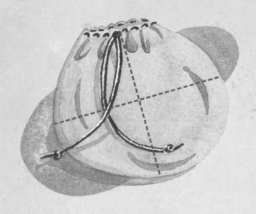

Making an Apothecary's Bag

What Do I Need?
A circle of metallic-looking fabric, about 12 inches (30 cm) in diameter
A circle of soft, felt fabric, about 9 inches (20 cm) in diameter
Needle and thread
Length of leather thong
A sprinkling of some dried chamomile
Some salt

When Do I Need to Do the Spell?
Any time you like

What Should I Do?
Put the two pieces of fabric together, and sew four lines that cross over each other, imagining all the great stuff that you will put in each pocket of the bag. This will be your special Apothecary's Bag into which you can put all your favorite spell ingredients. Sprinkle some salt and chamomile into each pocket before using the bag. Now, by putting your ingredients into this bag, you are making them even more powerful for your spell. Tie the bag closed with the leather thong.

Your Notes

Could you get all the ingredients? Yes ☐ No ☐
_____

If not, list the other ingredients that you have used.
_____

_____

When did you make the bag? _Time_ _____ _Day_ _____

What Phase of the Moon is it? _New Moon_ ☐ _Waxing_ ☐ _Full_ ☐ _Waning_ ☐

Did anything happen while you were making the bag?
_____

_____

_____

_____

What thoughts occurred to you?
_____

_____

_____

_____

Did anything odd happen after making the bag?
_____

_____

_____

_____

Finding Out Your Future Using Marbles

What Do I Need?

Six of your favorite marbles, of different colors or patterns

A black marble, bigger than the others

A special bag or your Apothecary's Bag (see page 26)

A blue-colored stone that looks like a sapphire

When Do I Need to Do the Spell?

Any time you like

What Should I Do?

Collect your marbles, and keep them in the bag overnight. Also include the blue stone, which is useful for encouraging truthfulness. The next day, roll the marbles out of the bag onto a level surface, preferably on the floor.

The big, black marble is your question, while your six small marbles represent a simple answer to your question, such as "Yes" or "No." Decide which small marble means what, keeping the marbles in the bag together until you need to ask a question.

To ask a question, hold the black marble in your hand and think of what you want to ask. Put the marble back in the bag with the others, and jiggle them about while you still think of your question. Roll the marbles out of the bag. The small marble that rolls closest to your black marble is the answer to your question.

Your Notes

Which color marble means the following to you:

1. "Yes" –

2. "No" –

You can add other answers, such as "*Wait*" or "*Do it immediately*":

3.

4.

5.

6.

What happened during the spell? What thoughts occurred to you?

Did anything odd happen after the spell?

Do you think your spell worked?

Celebrating Midsummer's Eve

What Do I Need?

A wreath made from branches

A group of friends who each bring a symbol of what they want to happen in
the next three months (for example, a toy house to represent a new home)

A ball of string, cut into small lengths

Name tags

A black marker pen

When Do I Need to Do the Spell?

On the evening of the summer solstice (21st–23rd of June in the Northern
Hemisphere; 21st–23rd of December in the Southern Hemisphere)

What Should I Do?

Sit in a circle with the wreath in the middle. Each person should have his or
her object and name tag. Go around the circle counterclockwise, letting each
person have a turn at tying his or her object and name tag to the wreath. As
each ties both things to the wreath, the following words should be said:

> Circle of branches,
> Circle of safety,
> Bring me my wish,
> A harvest of plenty.

Place the wreath in a sunny spot where it will not be disturbed.
See whose wish comes true first.

Your Notes

Could you get all the ingredients?   *Yes* ☐ *No* ☐

If not, list the other ingredients that you have used.

When did you do the spell?   *Time*   *Day*

What Phase of the Moon is it?   *New Moon* ☐ *Waxing* ☐ *Full* ☐ *Waning* ☐

What happened during the spell? What thoughts occurred to you?

Did anything odd happen after the spell?

Do you think your spell worked?

Creating Secret Invisible Messages

What Do I Need?
A small bowl
A lemon
A fine-tipped paintbrush
A piece of notepaper
An ordinary ballpoint pen

When Do I Need to Do the Spell?
Any time you like

What Should I Do?
With your ballpoint pen, write a simple note to a friend. Squeeze the lemon, gathering the juice in the small bowl. In between the lines of your note, paint a simple password or short secret message to your friend, using the paintbrush and lemon juice. Use a cotton swab to write the word or message if you don't like using a paintbrush. Your friend will be able to read the message if the paper is put near, but not too near, a source of heat, such as a heater or radiator. The secret writing will then turn brown.

Your Notes

Could you get all the ingredients?   *Yes* ☐ *No* ☐

If not, list the other ingredients that you have used.

Did the lemon juice work?

There are many recipes for invisible ink – when you find one, jot it down here.

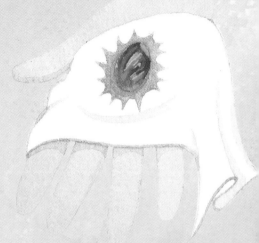

Making Yourself Appear Invisible

What Do I Need?

A piece of a special stone called an opal (this stone is usually available very
    cheaply as a sliver surrounded by a resin, making it look like a smooth
    stone). If you can't get an opal, try to get a small piece of bloodstone.
A clean, white or blue cotton handkerchief

When Do I Need to Do the Spell?

Any time you like

What Should I Do?

Hold the stone in your hand, and imagine that a blue light is coming from
within the stone. Imagine the light becoming stronger so that it is shining
around your hand. Continue imagining the light growing until the light is
shining around your whole body. This light will distract anyone trying to look
at you, giving you the opportunity to leave without being spotted. Carry the
stone with you, keeping it in the handkerchief or bag until you need it.

Your Notes

Could you get all the ingredients?   Yes ☐ No ☐

If not, list the other ingredients that you have used.

When did you do the spell?   *Time*   *Day*

What Phase of the Moon is it?   *New Moon* ☐ *Waxing* ☐ *Full* ☐ *Waning* ☐

What happened during the spell? What thoughts occurred to you?

Did anything odd happen after the spell?

Do you think your spell worked?

Celebrating Halloween

What Do I Need?
A fine, white silk handkerchief
A stiff piece of black paper or cardboard
A black pen
Three paper clips

When Do I Need to Do the Spell?
Try this at a Halloween party (usually held on the 31st of October, if you live in the Northern Hemisphere; or on the 30th of April, if you live in the Southern Hemisphere)

What Should I Do?
Draw a scary ghost on the white silk handkerchief. Wear a long-sleeved jacket. Bend one of the paper clips so that it is like a hook, then secure the other end to your handkerchief. Stuff the handkerchief up your right sleeve, folding it down so it doesn't bulk up your sleeve. Allow the hook of the paper clip to rest slightly outside your jacket. Roll the cardboard so that it is wide enough for you to pass your arm through it. Secure each end with a paper clip.

When ready to make a ghost appear from the empty roll of cardboard, pass your right arm through the roll, showing your audience that the roll is empty. Really, you are using the top paperclip of the roll to hook the "ghost" silk handkerchief from out of your right sleeve. Put the roll on its end on the table, and make a great show of being able to catch a ghost by pulling the silk handkerchief out of an empty roll of cardboard! Practice this in front of a mirror before trying it out on a live, "spirited" audience!

Your Notes

Could you get all the ingredients?   *Yes* ☐ *No* ☐

If not, list the other ingredients that you have used.

Were you able to do the magic trick to your satisfaction?

Did anything odd happen after the magic trick?

Are there any other spells that you would like to try during Halloween?

Write them down here.

Making a Wizard's Wand

What Do I Need?
A branch that has fallen on the forest or garden floor
Sandpaper
A length of copper wire
A pot of glue
A clear crystal with a point, or a pointy-shaped stone
A rounded purple crystal, or a couple of colorful feathers

When Do I Need to Do the Spell?
At New Moon

What Should I Do?
Find your branch, and sand it so that the wood is smooth. Tidy each end, then glue the pointed, clear crystal at one end and the rounded, purple crystal at the other end. If you haven't got the crystals, use a pointy stone that you have found lying around and that you like the look of at one end, and collect a couple of feathers and attach them to the other end. At the bottom of the wand (the end with the rounded purple stone or feathers), attach one end of the copper wire. Copper conducts magical energy. Twirl the wire around the shaft of the wand until you reach the top (the end with the pointy crystal or stone). Your wand is complete.

Your Notes

Could you get all the ingredients? *Yes* ☐ *No* ☐
_____

If not, list the other ingredients that you have used.
_____

_____

When did you make your wand? *Time*   *Day*
_____

What Phase of the Moon is it? *New Moon* ☐ *Waxing* ☐ *Full* ☐ *Waning* ☐

What happened while you were making your wand?
_____

_____

_____

_____

What thoughts occurred to you?
_____

_____

_____

_____

Did anything odd happen after making the wand?
_____

_____

_____

_____

Earthly Concerns

Spell of Plenty

What Do I Need?
Three small mirrors
Sticky tape or masking tape
Black marker pen
A pile of coins

When Do I Need to Do the Spell?
During the phase of the New Moon

What Should I Do?
Draw on the back of one mirror the symbol of a dollar sign ($). On the other two, draw a circle with a dot in the middle (the occult symbol of success), while on the back of the third one, draw a downward-pointing triangle with a bar across the middle. Secure the three mirrors so that they form a triangle using the sticky/masking tape. Make sure that the mirrors are facing inward. In the space in the middle, pile up all the coins you currently have – the mirrors will reflect the amount to infinity.

Your Notes

Could you get all the ingredients?   *Yes* ☐ *No* ☐

If not, list the other ingredients that you have used.

When did you do the spell?   *Time*   *Day*

What Phase of the Moon is it?   *New Moon* ☐ *Waxing* ☐ *Full* ☐ *Waning* ☐

What happened during the spell? What thoughts occurred to you?

Did anything odd happen after the spell?

Do you think your spell worked?

Finding the Dragon's Treasure

What Do I Need?
A stick that branches into two
Two lengths of copper wire
Sandpaper
A red marker pen

When Do I Need to Do the Spell?
During the phase of the New Moon

What Should I Do?
Prepare your stick, which will become your "dowsing" rod to find buried treasure. Find a branch that forks into two. Make sure that you do not tear the branch from a tree for a magical purpose, because its flow of magical current will be seriously disturbed by this violent action. On the main part of the stick, draw a picture of a fierce dragon with your red pen.

Coil a length of copper wire from the right-hand forked branch up to the top of the central branch, and do the same on the left-hand side. Hold the branch by the fork, and experiment with feeling a "current" through the branch. Bury a coin in the ground and point the stick at it to gauge how the "current" feels. You will soon become sensitive to the messages that your "dowsing" rod is sending you, so that you can go hunt for buried treasure.

Your Notes

Could you get all the ingredients?   Yes ☐   No ☐

If not, list the other ingredients that you have used.

When did you do the spell?   *Time*   *Day*

What Phase of the Moon is it?   *New Moon* ☐   *Waxing* ☐   *Full* ☐   *Waning* ☐

What happened during the spell? What thoughts occurred to you?

Did anything odd happen after the spell?

Do you think your spell worked?

Catching Sight of the Rabbit Good Luck Spell

What Do I Need?
Silver coin

When Do I Need to Do the Spell?
During the phase of the New Moon

What Should I Do?
Visit a place where you know you will see rabbits. Have the silver coin in a pocket on your left-hand side. This side is linked to your magical abilities and intuition, so it is a good idea to carry any spell ingredients in your left hand or on your left-hand side. Sit quietly, thinking of all the luck that you have had in your life so far. Keep your eyes open for your first glimpse of a rabbit. As soon as you see one, take the silver coin out of your pocket as quickly as possible, and show it to the New Moon. The quicker you are, the luckier you shall be!

Your Notes

Could you get all the ingredients?   *Yes* ☐ *No* ☐
_____

If not, list the other ingredients that you have used.
_____

_____

When did you do the spell?   *Time*   *Day*
_____

What Phase of the Moon is it?   *New Moon* ☐ *Waxing* ☐ *Full* ☐ *Waning* ☐

What happened during the spell? What thoughts occurred to you?
_____

_____

_____

_____

Did anything odd happen after the spell?
_____

_____

_____

_____

Do you think your spell worked?
_____

_____

Merlin's Good Luck Potion

What Do I Need?

A clear bottle with a stopper
Enough cola to fill the bottle
A gold-colored coin with a hole in the middle

When Do I Need to Do the Spell?

During the phase of the New Moon

What Should I Do?

Measure out the liquid into the clear bottle. Make sure that the neck of the bottle is wide enough to allow you to throw your coin into the liquid. When ready, hold the coin in your hand, and think of all the lucky things that have happened to you, as well as all the luck that you would like to have in the future. Plunge the coin into the liquid, empowering the potion to bring you good luck. Stopper the bottle, and place it somewhere up high near a window, for instance on a bookshelf.

Your Notes

Could you get all the ingredients? Yes ☐ No ☐

If not, list the other ingredients that you have used.

When did you do the spell? *Time*   *Day*

What Phase of the Moon is it? *New Moon* ☐ *Waxing* ☐ *Full* ☐ *Waning* ☐

What happened during the spell? What thoughts occurred to you?

Did anything odd happen after the spell?

Do you think your spell worked?

Making a Talisman for Success

What Do I Need?
A gold disc, (either metal or gold-colored cardboard cut into
  a circle, about 2 inches (5 cm) in diameter
A black marker pen
A gold drawstring bag (with an optional leather thong attached)

When Do I Need to Do the Spell?
During the height of the sun's powers during the day, such as noon

What Should I Do?
Draw on one side of the gold disc the following grouping of numbers:

6	32	3	34	35	1
7	11	27	28	8	30
19	14	16	15	23	24
18	20	22	21	17	13
25	29	10	9	26	12
36	5	33	4	2	31

These numbers, arranged in a square, will attract the powers of the Sun to
you, especially if, on the other side of the gold disc, you write your full name.
Pop the disc into the gold-colored bag and either wear it around your neck or
carry it in a left-hand pocket.

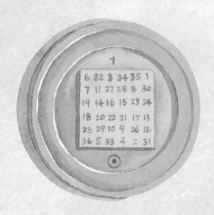

Your Notes

Could you get all the ingredients?   *Yes* ☐ *No* ☐

If not, list the other ingredients that you have used.

When did you do the spell?   *Time*   *Day*

What Phase of the Moon is it?   *New Moon* ☐ *Waxing* ☐ *Full* ☐ *Waning* ☐

What happened during the spell? What thoughts occurred to you?

Did anything odd happen after the spell?

Do you think your spell worked?

Getting What You Need Spell

What Do I Need?
A piece of paper, about 6 inches (15 cm) long and 4 inches (10 cm) wide
A gold-colored wire paper clip
A silver-colored wire paper clip

When Do I Need to Do the Spell?
During the phase of the New Moon or Waxing Moon

What Should I Do?
Write what you want or need at the moment on the piece of paper. Fold the note into thirds without creasing the edges. Secure one of the end thirds to the middle third with your gold clip. This clip represents the things you feel you need. Then secure the other end third to the middle third with your silver paper clip, which represents you. Now, imagine that you are straightening the path between you and your needs as you gently pull the piece of paper out of its folds. The spell starts when the paper clips magically connect!

Your Notes

Could you get all the ingredients? *Yes* ☐ *No* ☐
_____

If not, list the other ingredients that you have used.
_____

_____

When did you do the spell? *Time*   *Day*
_____

What Phase of the Moon is it? *New Moon* ☐ *Waxing* ☐ *Full* ☐ *Waning* ☐

What happened during the spell? What thoughts occurred to you?
_____

_____

_____

_____

_____

Did anything odd happen after the spell?
_____

_____

_____

_____

Do you think your spell worked?
_____

_____

Making Fairy Gold

What Do I Need?

Four or five gold coins of varying sizes (these can be metal or
  gold-covered chocolate coins)
A pin or nail strong enough and long enough to hold the coins in place
  (if metal, rivet the coins together so that the pin or nail is not visible)

When Do I Need to Do the Spell?

Any time you like

What Should I Do?

In the olden days, stories abounded of a Wizard paying his way by giving an
innkeeper "fairy gold." It was only after the Wizard was long gone that the
innkeeper realized that the gold was not real. There is a trick that can be done
to keep your friends guessing how much money you have in your hand. This
simple trick is to rivet or pin together four or five coins so that the top coin is
the largest, giving the impression, when the coins are all fanned out, that you
have four or five large coins. However, you are then able to hide
the coins behind the one big coin, so that it seems that you only have one
coin in your hand.

Your Notes

Could you get all the ingredients?   *Yes* ☐ *No* ☐
_____

If not, list the other ingredients that you have used.
_____

_____

Is there any way you can improve or make this trick work better?
_____

_____

_____

_____

_____

List here any other coin tricks that you enjoy doing.
_____

_____

_____

_____

_____

_____

_____

_____

Making a Lucky Amulet Bag

What Do I Need?
A green drawstring bag
A stone with a naturally occurring hole
A green feather
Any other items that seem lucky to you

When Do I Need to Do the Spell?
During the phase of the New or Waxing Moon

What Should I Do?
Put the stone and the feather into the bag. For the next 28 days, put into the bag anything that seems lucky to you. For example, if you find a four-leaf clover, put that in the bag. If you win some marbles, put one into the bag. If you find some money (that cannot be returned), put some of it into the bag. These items all build up a powerful energy of good luck for you, as well as help you to realize how lucky you really are already!

Your Notes

Could you get all the ingredients?   *Yes* ☐   *No* ☐

If not, list the other ingredients that you have used.

When did you do the spell?   *Time*   *Day*

What Phase of the Moon is it?   *New Moon* ☐   *Waxing* ☐   *Full* ☐   *Waning* ☐

What happened during the spell? What thoughts occurred to you?

Did anything odd happen after the spell?

Do you think your spell worked?

The Serpent of Success Spell

What Do I Need?
Clay that can be rolled out into a thin strip
about 12–15 inches (30–45 cm) long
Glue that can secure glass to clay
A green marble

When Do I Need to Do the Spell?
During a Waxing Moon

What Should I Do?
Roll out some clay so that you have a long strip. Coil one end onto itself to create a center. Imagine that this section is your starting point of success. Keep coiling the strip around this center, making the spiral grow bigger. As you are coiling, imagine that you are capturing more and more success into your life. When you have finished the coil, sprinkle the spiral "serpent" with salty water (using your Wizardly chalice, if you have one – see pages 14–15). Leave the serpent to dry. When the clay feels dry to the touch, glue the green marble in the middle. This is the serpent's eye, attracting success to you. Place the serpent on your special spell table (see pages 10–11), or on your desk at home.

Your Notes

Could you get all the ingredients? *Yes* ☐ *No* ☐

If not, list the other ingredients that you have used.

When did you do the spell? *Time*   *Day*

What Phase of the Moon is it? *New Moon* ☐ *Waxing* ☐ *Full* ☐ *Waning* ☐

What happened during the spell? What thoughts occurred to you?

Did anything odd happen after the spell?

Do you think your spell worked?

Rune for Making Wishes Come True

What Do I Need?
A flat stone that fits in your pocket
A black marker pen

When Do I Need to Do the Spell?
Any time you like

What Should I Do?
First, find your flat stone. Go out specially to find a stone for this spell. Before going on a walk, imagine that you are searching for a precious stone that will help you obtain all your wishes. When you are on the walk, keep an eye out for just the right stone for this spell. If you don't find it the first time, do not worry. You may need to take several days to find just the right one. When you have found the right stone, draw the following rune to help your wishes come true:

Keep this stone in your pocket when you are casting any spells.

Your Notes

Could you get all the ingredients?   *Yes* ☐ *No* ☐

If not, list the other ingredients that you have used.

When did you do the spell?   *Time*   *Day*

What Phase of the Moon is it?   *New Moon* ☐ *Waxing* ☐ *Full* ☐ *Waning* ☐

What happened during the spell? What thoughts occurred to you?

Did anything odd happen after the spell?

Do you think your spell worked?

An Air of Confidence

Special Mirror Spell for Confidence

What Do I Need?
Red, orange, and yellow glass beads and stones
Two pieces of a stone called "cat's eye" [optional]
Glue
A mirror with a frame that you can decorate (preferably gold-colored)

When Do I Need to Do the Spell?
During the phase of the New or Waxing Moon

What Should I Do?
Decorate the frame of the mirror with all the colorful beads and stones. These colors are symbolic of the sun, and of feelings of success. In the middle of the frame, at the top, you may wish to glue the two "cat's eye" stones, which not only give you a sense of confidence, but will also bring you luck with people and money.

Your Notes

Could you get all the ingredients?   *Yes* ☐ *No* ☐

If not, list the other ingredients that you have used.

When did you do the spell?   *Time*   *Day*

What Phase of the Moon is it?   *New Moon* ☐ *Waxing* ☐ *Full* ☐ *Waning* ☐

What happened during the spell? What thoughts occurred to you?

Did anything odd happen after the spell?

Do you think your spell worked?

Dream Advice Spell

What Do I Need?
Peppermint toothpaste
A journal (or your Wizards Handbook)
Your favorite pen

When Do I Need to Do the Spell?
Just before going to bed

What Should I Do?
Just before going to bed, brush your teeth with your special peppermint-flavored toothpaste. Peppermint is well known for helping you to have good dreams and for helping you to remember your dreams. After brushing your teeth, sit in bed for a few moments with your journal or this Handbook and your pen. What would you like advice about? Write down the questions you would like to have answered. Say the following charm, as you go to sleep:

> "I wish I may, I wish I might,
> Have a dream to answer me right."

Upon waking, write down all the dreams you can remember.
Your answer will be among your dreams!

Your Notes

Could you get all the ingredients?   *Yes* ☐ *No* ☐

If not, list the other ingredients that you have used.

When did you do the spell?   *Time*   *Day*

What Phase of the Moon is it?   *New Moon* ☐ *Waxing* ☐ *Full* ☐ *Waning* ☐

What happened during the spell? What thoughts occurred to you?

Did anything odd happen after the spell?

Do you think your spell worked?

65

Finding Lost Stuff Spell

What Do I Need?
A piece of paper
A black pen

When Do I Need to Do the Spell?
Any time you like

What Should I Do?
On one side of the piece of paper, write or draw what you have lost.
Concentrate on the object. Turn over the piece of paper and draw a tiny circle.
This is your lost object. Pretend that you are the object, and that the object
has eyes. Imagine that you are looking around you, and draw what you see
around you or answer the questions on opposite page.

Your Notes

Is it dark or light around you [as the lost object]?   *Yes* ☒ *No* ☐

Are you under something?   *Yes* ☒ *No* ☐

Are you on top of something?   *Yes* ☐ *No* ☒

Are you outside ~~or inside~~?   *Yes* ☐ *No* ☒

Are you where you are supposed to be?   *Yes* ☐ *No* ☒

Are you at home?   *Yes* ☒ *No* ☐

Are you at school?   *Yes* ☐ *No* ☒

Are you at a friend's place?   *Yes* ☐ *No* ☒

What can you see around you?   Togs

Where am I?   Right in my room

Increase Your Brain Power Spell

$$2 + 2 = 4$$

What Do I Need?
A piece of paper
A black pen

When Do I Need to Do the Spell?
Any time you like
Try this out on your friends!

What Should I Do?
Pick a four-digit number (with no repeated numbers), such as 7263. Scramble the numbers (for example, 3627), and subtract the scrambled number from your original number (for example, 7263 − 3627 = 3636). Add up the four digits of the answer (for example, 3 + 6 + 3 + 6 = 18). Now, add up the two remaining digits (for example, 1 + 8 = 9). No matter what four numbers you use originally, the answer will always be 9!

Wizardly spell tip: Nine is a very important number in magic. To cast a spell, a Wizard may choose to say a charm nine times or walk nine times around in a circle before settling to do the rest of the spell.

$$2 + 2 = 4$$

Your Notes

Write down any other of your favorite number tricks. You will be amazed how many feature the number nine!

_____

_____

_____

_____

_____

_____

_____

_____

_____

_____

_____

$$2 + 2 = 4$$

Fly Like An Eagle Spell

What Do I Need?
A picture of an eagle
A gray and white feather, or a brown one
A compass to show you where East lies (the
    direction that relates to the element of Air)

When Do I Need to Do the Spell?
Any time you like

What Should I Do?
Find a comfortable space where you can be alone for a while, such as your
bedroom or at your spell table (see pages 10–11). Use your compass to find
out which way is East. Cast a circle around your space (see pages 12–13), and
sit in the circle facing East with your picture of an eagle held in your right
hand and the feather held in your left hand. Look at your picture of the eagle,
imagining that you are feeling a breeze coming from the East. Feel it ruffling
your feathers, and that you are slowly becoming airborne. Focus hard on the
feeling of flying, enjoying the sensation of being free from gravity for a while!
When ready, let go of the picture and feather, and put your hands on the
ground – you are no longer an eagle.

Your Notes

Could you get all the ingredients?   *Yes* ☐ *No* ☐

If not, list the other ingredients that you have used.

When did you do the spell?   *Time*   *Day*

What Phase of the Moon is it?   *New Moon* ☐ *Waxing* ☐ *Full* ☐ *Waning* ☐

What happened during the spell? What thoughts occurred to you?

Did anything odd happen after the spell?

Do you think your spell worked?

A Batty Tallness Spell

What Do I Need?
A purple cord that measures about 6-and-a-half feet (about 2 m)
A piece of black cardboard
A white pen
A wooden box

When Do I Need to Do the Spell?
During the phase of the Full Moon

What Should I Do?
Step on one end of the cord with your heel, pulling the cord up to your head. Make a knot. Continue pulling the cord up past your head, tying a knot at the point to which you would like to grow. You may want to do this spell in front of a full-length mirror. Measure the new height, writing it on one side of the black piece of cardboard. On the other side, draw a picture of a bat while you are imagining the bat flying above your head at the new height that you wish to be. Put the cord and the picture of the bat in the wooden box, and keep it where the Moon will shine on it.

Your Notes

Could you get all the ingredients? *Yes* ☐ *No* ☐

If not, list the other ingredients that you have used.

When did you do the spell? *Time*   *Day*

What Phase of the Moon is it? *New Moon* ☐ *Waxing* ☐ *Full* ☐ *Waning* ☐

What happened during the spell? What thoughts occurred to you?

Did anything odd happen after the spell?

Do you think your spell worked?

Special Cosmic Spell For Help

What Do I Need?
A silver drawstring bag
A gold-colored disc for the Sun
A piece of moonstone for the Moon
Four almonds for Mercury
A piece of copper for Venus
A piece of dried ginger for Mars
The letter "F" for Saturn
On a piece of deep-blue fabric, draw the following symbol for Jupiter:

When Do I Need to Do the Spell?
Any time you like

What Should I Do?
Collect all the ingredients, asking each celestial body to give you the help that you need. Put all the items in the drawstring bag, and carry the bag with you until you receive the help you need or are given guidance that will help you out of trouble.

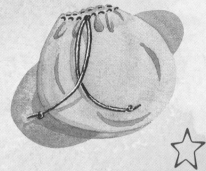

Your Notes

Could you get all the ingredients?   Yes ☐ No ☐

If not, list the other ingredients that you have used.

When did you do the spell?   *Time*   *Day*

What Phase of the Moon is it?   *New Moon* ☐ *Waxing* ☐ *Full* ☐ *Waning* ☐

What happened during the spell? What thoughts occurred to you?

Did anything odd happen after the spell?

Do you think your spell worked?

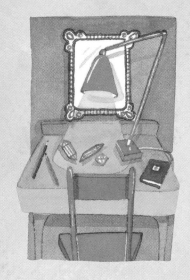

A Getting Noticed Spell

What Do I Need?
A flat surface where you do your homework (a study desk at home)
A small mirror
A clear quartz crystal

When Do I Need to Do the Spell?
During the phase of the New Moon or Waxing Moon

What Should I Do?
Sit in your chair at your desk as usual, and position the mirror and crystal directly opposite where you are sitting. It would also be a good idea to place your table lamp in this position as well! In ancient Chinese beliefs, this area relates to your fame and acknowledgement. By placing these items in this area of your desk, you will encourage positive energy to help you get noticed!

Your Notes

Could you get all the ingredients? *Yes* ☐ *No* ☐

If not, list the other ingredients that you have used.

When did you do the spell? *Time*   *Day*

What Phase of the Moon is it? *New Moon* ☐ *Waxing* ☐ *Full* ☐ *Waning* ☐

What happened during the spell? What thoughts occurred to you?

Did anything odd happen after the spell?

Do you think your spell worked?

Finding a Special Wizard Pet

What Do I Need?
A batch of pictures of your favorite animals

When Do I Need to Do the Spell?
During the phase of the New Moon or Waxing Moon

What Should I Do?
Sort though your animal pictures, choosing the one animal that you would most like to have as a wizardly pet. Examine the picture closely, while you imagine how that animal would be and how you would be together. When ready, prop up the picture on a window where it will catch the light of the Moon. Keep the picture at the window for three nights, keeping an eye out for any new creatures in your neighborhood, as your wizardly pet may come to visit in one of its many forms!

Your Notes

Could you get all the ingredients?   *Yes* ☑ *No* ☐

If not, list the other ingredients that you have used.

When did you do the spell?   *Time* 4:00PM *Day* Feb 1st. 2009

What Phase of the Moon is it?   *New Moon* ☐ *Waxing* ☐ *Full* ☐ *Waning* ☐

What happened during the spell? What thoughts occurred to you? I began
to make up a name and life story for
my horse.

Did anything odd happen after the spell?

Do you think your spell worked? Yes

Fire of the Dragon's Breath

Magic for Making Your Wishes Come True

What Do I Need?
A red candle with the wick cut off
A teaspoon of sunflower oil
A pin
A piece of red fabric big enough to wrap the candle

When Do I Need to Do the Spell?
During the phase of the New Moon or Waxing Moon

What Should I Do?
Along the length of the red candle, write down your wish, using the pin. Use as few words as possible when describing your wish. For example, write the words "Money," "Holiday," "Baseball bat," or "Bike." To get rid of the wax shavings, rub the oil into the candle, imagining that your wish has come true. Cut off the candle wick, and do not light the candle. Wrap the candle in the red fabric, and bury it somewhere outside where it won't be seen. However, make sure that it is as close to the front door, gate, or path as possible.

Remember: Do not light the candle.

Your Notes

Could you get all the ingredients?   *Yes* ☐   *No* ☐

If not, list the other ingredients that you have used.

When did you do the spell?   *Time*   *Day*

What Phase of the Moon is it?   *New Moon* ☐ *Waxing* ☐ *Full* ☐ *Waning* ☐

What happened during the spell? What thoughts occurred to you?

Did anything odd happen after the spell?

Do you think your spell worked?

A Spell for Strengthening Your Will

What Do I Need?
A piece of paper
A red pen
A length of red string
A piece of red agate or a red marble

When Do I Need to Do the Spell?
Any time you like

What Should I Do?
Hold the red stone or marble in your hand (your left hand if you write with your right hand, or your right hand if you write with your left hand). Squeeze as hard as you can, while feeling that your will is as strong as the stone or marble. With the other hand, write on the piece of paper nine times the following words with your red pen:

"I wish to have the willpower to [insert what you want to do or finish]."

Roll up the piece of paper as tightly as you can, then tie it with the red string. Place the rolled paper with the stone or marble somewhere in your room where the noonday sun reaches. Leave the items there for three days.

Your Notes

Could you get all the ingredients?   *Yes* ☐ *No* ☐
_____

If not, list the other ingredients that you have used.
_____

_____

When did you do the spell?   *Time*   *Day*
_____

What Phase of the Moon is it?   *New Moon* ☐ *Waxing* ☐ *Full* ☐ *Waning* ☐

What happened during the spell? What thoughts occurred to you?
_____

_____

_____

_____

_____

Did anything odd happen after the spell?
_____

_____

_____

_____

Do you think your spell worked?
_____

_____

Smoke from the Cauldron Spell

What Do I Need?
A good imagination!

When Do I Need to Do the Spell?
Any time you like

What Should I Do?
When you see smoke coming from a chimney or candle, or steam from a kettle or bathtub full of hot water, practice your skills of imagination. Imagination, also called "visualization," is one of the most important tools of a Wizard. See if you can make the smoke look like something. At first, you may see all sorts of funny shapes. After some practice, ask a question and see if you can see shapes forming in the smoke or steam that suggest an answer.

Your Notes

Could you get all the ingredients?   *Yes* ☐ *No* ☐

If not, list the other ingredients that you have used.

When did you do the spell?   *Time*   *Day*

What Phase of the Moon is it?   *New Moon* ☐ *Waxing* ☐ *Full* ☐ *Waning* ☐

What happened during the spell? What thoughts occurred to you?

Did anything odd happen after the spell?

Do you think your spell worked?

Dragon Spell for Empowering Your Wizard's Wand

What Do I Need?
Some red and black paint
Red and black marker pens
Red cardboard, scissors, glue [optional]
A pinch of salt
A cup of water

When Do I Need to Do the Spell?
Any time you like

What Should I Do?
Make your wand according to the instructions on page 38. Mix the salt with the water, then sprinkle the salty water over the wand. Go outside and plunge the wand into the earth, saying the following words:

"Powers of the Elements, Empower my Magic Wand."

Bring the wand back inside. In a special space where you will not be interrupted, decorate the wand with red and black, perhaps painting dragon scales along the length of the wand, or a long, curvy dragon. You may even wish to attach a pair of dragon wings to the wand. If you can find red feathers, these are a great item to attach to your wand to attract success and good fortune to your spells.

Your Notes

Could you get all the ingredients? Yes ☐ No ☐

If not, list the other ingredients that you have used.

When did you do the spell? *Time*   *Day*

What Phase of the Moon is it? *New Moon* ☐ *Waxing* ☐ *Full* ☐ *Waning* ☐

What happened during the spell? What thoughts occurred to you?

Did anything odd happen after the spell?

Do you think your spell worked?

Glowing Hands Healing Spell

What Do I Need?
Just your hands!

When Do I Need to Do the Spell?
Any time you feel unwell or unhappy

What Should I Do?
Focus on your breathing. Breathe in for a count of three, and breathe out for a count of four. Imagine that you can breathe in blue light that travels down to your hands. Imagine that this blue light is a healing, warm, and comforting light. Feel your hands throbbing with this light and healing energy. If you have a stomach ache, put your hands on your stomach and rub your hands in a clockwise direction three times, and then in a counterclockwise direction three times. Do this until you are given some medicine to further help your healing.

Your Notes

Could you get all the ingredients?   *Yes* ☐ *No* ☐

If not, list the other ingredients that you have used.

When did you do the spell?   *Time*   *Day*

What Phase of the Moon is it?   *New Moon* ☐ *Waxing* ☐ *Full* ☐ *Waning* ☐

What happened during the spell? What thoughts occurred to you?

Did anything odd happen after the spell?

Do you think your spell worked?

Monster Protection Spell

What Do I Need?
A pair of unwashed socks
Two pieces of scrap paper, which will be scrunched up
A red pen

When Do I Need to Do the Spell?
Any time you feel the need for protection

What Should I Do?
On a piece of paper, draw a circle, making sure that the ends meet. The circle is a powerful symbol of protection. Draw a stick figure in the middle of the circle. Inside the circle but above the stick figure, write your name; below the figure, write the word "Protection." Outside the circle, write the names of or draw all the monsters that scare you. Do the same drawing on the other piece of paper. Scrunch up the pieces of paper, putting one in each sock so that the sock is filled out. Hang or put the socks near the doorway to your bedroom. This should stop the worst of the monsters from coming in!

Your Notes

Could you get all the ingredients? *Yes* ☐ *No* ☐
_____

If not, list the other ingredients that you have used.
_____

_____

When did you do the spell? *Time*   *Day*
_____

What Phase of the Moon is it? *New Moon* ☐ *Waxing* ☐ *Full* ☐ *Waning* ☐

What happened during the spell? What thoughts occurred to you?
_____

_____

_____

_____

Did anything odd happen after the spell?
_____

_____

_____

_____

Do you think your spell worked?
_____

_____

Protecting Your Home from Ghouls and Goblins

What Do I Need?
Two sticks made from pine
A pinch of salt
A bowl of water
Some fresh dill

When Do I Need to Do the Spell?
Any time you feel that there is some strange energy in your room or home

What Should I Do?
Take your two pine sticks with you as you walk into the room or area that feels as if it has some bad energy; for example, if the temperature in the room is much lower than the rest of the house, or the colors seem dark and muddy, or the sound seems unclear. Go to each corner of the space and clap the two sticks together until the energy feels clearer (for example, if the colors or sounds in the room become sharper). When you have finished, get the bowl of water and sprinkle a pinch of salt into it. Use a small bunch of fresh dill to lightly sprinkle the salty water around the room.

Your Notes

Could you get all the ingredients?   Yes ☐   No ☐

If not, list the other ingredients that you have used.

When did you do the spell?   *Time*   *Day*

What Phase of the Moon is it?   *New Moon* ☐   *Waxing* ☐   *Full* ☐   *Waning* ☐

What happened during the spell? What thoughts occurred to you?

Did anything odd happen after the spell?

Do you think your spell worked?

Casting a Protective Castle Around Your Stuff

What Do I Need?
Four flat rocks that all fit into the palm of your hand
A black permanent marker pen

When Do I Need to Do the Spell?
Any time you need to protect your stuff

What Should I Do?
On each stone, draw the following symbols, which represent the four Elements
– Earth,   Air,   Fire,   and Water

If you are protecting your stuff at home, place the stones around your things, imagining that each stone is the cornerstone of a huge castle with fluorescent green or blue walls that magically rise up when you say the following words:

"Powers of the Elements, Rise up the Walls of Protection."

If you are doing this spell to protect your schoolbag or your locker, just keep the four stones in each corner of your bag or locker and simply say the words of protection to create a castle stronghold to discourage anyone from taking or looking at your stuff.

Your Notes

Could you get all the ingredients?   *Yes* ☐ *No* ☐

_____

If not, list the other ingredients that you have used.

_____

_____

When did you do the spell?   *Time* _____   *Day* _____

What Phase of the Moon is it?   *New Moon* ☐ *Waxing* ☐ *Full* ☐ *Waning* ☐

What happened during the spell? What thoughts occurred to you?

_____

_____

_____

_____

_____

Did anything odd happen after the spell?

_____

_____

_____

_____

Do you think your spell worked?

_____

_____

Wishing on a Bonfire

What Do I Need?

A bonfire that has already been started (do not start one yourself unless you
  have responsible adult supervision)

A piece of paper that has your wish written on it

A willow branch

Red ribbon or string

When Do I Need to Do the Spell?

When the bonfire is burning at its brightest

What Should I Do?

Before going to the bonfire, write your wish on a piece of paper, imagining
that your wish has come true already. Roll the paper around your stick of
willow, and tie it with some red ribbon or red string. Willow is a very magical
wood, which can be purchased commercially or can be found on the ground.
Never cut a piece from a living tree. When the bonfire is burning at its
brightest, throw the stick into the flames, and say the wish that you have
written on the piece of paper.

Your Notes

Could you get all the ingredients? Yes ☐ No ☐

If not, list the other ingredients that you have used.

When did you do the spell? *Time*   *Day*

What Phase of the Moon is it? *New Moon* ☐ *Waxing* ☐ *Full* ☐ *Waning* ☐

What happened during the spell? What thoughts occurred to you?

Did anything odd happen after the spell?

Do you think your spell worked?

Making a Splash

Spells by the Seashore

What Do I Need?
A bunch of shells that you like
A circle of sand with a gap through which a wave can enter

When Do I Need to Do the Spell?
Any time you like

What Should I Do?
At the edge of the tide line, make a large circle by drawing it with a stick, leaving a gap through which a wave can enter. Build up the sides of the circle with a small wall of sand, and decorate the walls with all the shells and objects that you have found by the seashore. Watch the tide, and when the water comes up and enters your circle of sand, quickly make a wish. Imagine that what you wish for is carried into your circle of life by the tide.

Wizardly spell tip: When you find a shell that you like, always thank the ocean for presenting you with a present from the sea.

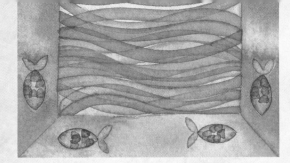

Your Notes

Could you get all the ingredients? *Yes* ☐ *No* ☐

If not, list the other ingredients that you have used.

When did you do the spell? *Time*   *Day*

What Phase of the Moon is it? *New Moon* ☐ *Waxing* ☐ *Full* ☐ *Waning* ☐

What happened during the spell? What thoughts occurred to you?

Did anything odd happen after the spell?

Do you think your spell worked?

Gathering Magical Dew Drops

What Do I Need?
A small jar with a lid
A black permanent marker pen

When Do I Need to Do the Spell?
At dawn

What Should I Do?
At dawn, preferably during summer, go
outside with your small jar, which has
been thoroughly cleaned and dried. Go
to each plant outside that has dew still
clinging to its leaves or petals, and gently
shake some of the dew into your jar. Do
this until you feel tired. On the following
night, leave the jar in a window that catches the
Moon's light, letting the moonlight infuse the dew with the
Moon's magical powers. Use this potion to sprinkle around your room
for protection or on some of your spell ingredients to heighten their
magical powers.

Wizardly spell tip: The most potent dew is collected on the dawn after
Midsummer's Eve (summer solstice).

Your Notes

When did you collect the dew?   *Time*   *Day*

What Phase of the Moon is it? *New Moon* ☐ *Waxing* ☐ *Full* ☐ *Waning* ☐

What happened while collecting the dew?

What thoughts occurred to you?

Did anything odd happen after collecting the dew?

Do you think your spell worked?

Spell for Making Friends Easily

What Do I Need?
A silver bowl half filled with fresh water
A wooden spoon
A sprinkle of salt or some magical
    dew (see page 102)

When Do I Need to Do the Spell?
During the phase of the New Moon or Waxing Moon

What Should I Do?
Place the silver bowl on a low table and sprinkle the salt and (if you have some) two drops of magical dew into it. Swirl the water with the wooden spoon to mix the salt and dew. Swirl the water in a clockwise direction, feeling how easily the spoon moves through the water. Imagine that the salt in the water is cleansing any bad luck you have had in making friends. Also, imagine that the easy way the spoon moves through the bowl of water is now how easy it will be for you to communicate with people and to make friends. When you have finished, throw out the water onto the earth, and imagine that your spell has become reality.

Your Notes

Could you get all the ingredients?   *Yes* ☐ *No* ☐

If not, list the other ingredients that you have used.

When did you do the spell?   *Time*   *Day*

What Phase of the Moon is it?   *New Moon* ☐ *Waxing* ☐ *Full* ☐ *Waning* ☐

What happened during the spell? What thoughts occurred to you?

Did anything odd happen after the spell?

Do you think your spell worked?

Making Your Own Wishing Well

What Do I Need?
A medium-sized flowerpot
Some plastic to line the bottom
    and sides of the pot
River pebbles, enough to fill the
    bottom of the pot and to line
    the walls of the pot
Water to fill the flowerpot
Some gold-colored coins

When Do I Need to Do the Spell?
Any time you like

What Should I Do?
Choose a spot in the garden or a safe space in an area where you are growing some indoor plants for your wishing well. Put your flowerpot in a place where you can leave it permanently. Cover the bottom of the flowerpot with plastic, then pile in enough river pebbles to fill the bottom of the pot and to line the walls. Fill the pot with water. Whenever you want to make a wish, hold a gold-colored coin in your hand until the coin is warm from the heat of your hand. Make a wish, then throw the coin in the water.

Wizardly spell tip: have some other pot plants, such as thyme, near your wishing well to increase its psychic power.

Your Notes

Could you get all the ingredients? *Yes* ☐ *No* ☐

If not, list the other ingredients that you have used.

When did you do the spell? *Time*   *Day*

What Phase of the Moon is it? *New Moon* ☐ *Waxing* ☐ *Full* ☐ *Waning* ☐

What happened during the spell? What thoughts occurred to you?

Did anything odd happen after the spell?

Do you think your spell worked?

Checking Under the Bed Spell

What Do I Need?
A pinch of salt mixed with the following herbs of magical protection:

> pepper
>
> parsley
>
> dill
>
> rosemary

A small bowl

A small white muslin or cotton bag and a length of string

When Do I Need to Do the Spell?
During daylight hours and before you go to bed

What Should I Do?
In a small bowl, mix the salt with the four herbs. These herbs can be dried or fresh; you only need a pinch of each. Put the mixture into the white bag and tie closed the bag with some string. During the day, clean or vacuum under your bed or get someone to help you. Clear out all the stuff under your bed, as all the things under there will stagnate the magical energy flowing around you, and can make you have bad dreams. Before you go to bed, look under the bed, tossing in the small white bag of protection herbs. This bag will cleanse any negative energy already present, and help to prevent negative energy from collecting under your bed.

Your Notes

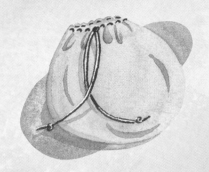

Could you get all the ingredients?   Yes ☐ No ☐

If not, list the other ingredients that you have used.

When did you do the spell?   *Time*   *Day*

What Phase of the Moon is it?   *New Moon* ☐ *Waxing* ☐ *Full* ☐ *Waning* ☐

What happened during the spell? What thoughts occurred to you?

Did anything odd happen after the spell?

Do you think your spell worked?

Clearing Unhappiness from Your Home

What Do I Need?
A handful of fresh rose petals and lavender
Water
A pinch of salt
A small silver-colored bowl
A piece of tiger's eye
A piece of carnelian

When Do I Need to Do the Spell?
This spell is particularly effective after a big argument

What Should I Do?
Fill the bowl half full of water, sprinkling in some rose petals and lavender. Go to the room or space where the argument happened. Lightly sprinkle the rose and lavender water over the door leading to the area, as well as over the windows. Clap in each corner and over any chairs and furniture with fabric on it. Throw the water into the garden or on some ground nearby. Dry the bowl and fill it with the remainder of the petals and lavender. Also include the tiger's eye, a great stone for getting rid of anger, and carnelian, a stone that attracts justice. Put the bowl near the entrance of the room to encourage more harmony in your home.

Your Notes

Could you get all the ingredients?   *Yes* ☐ *No* ☐

If not, list the other ingredients that you have used.

When did you do the spell?   *Time*   *Day*

What Phase of the Moon is it?   *New Moon* ☐ *Waxing* ☐ *Full* ☐ *Waning* ☐

What happened during the spell? What thoughts occurred to you?

Did anything odd happen after the spell?

Do you think your spell worked?

Spell for Protection Against Evil Wizards

What Do I Need?
A small cake of white soap
A pin

When Do I Need to Do the Spell?
During the phase of the Full Moon

What Should I Do?
Draw the following symbol of the Eye of Horus on one side of the cake of soap, using your pin:

Make the pattern as deep as possible. This is excellent protection against the evil eye, and has been used by Wizards since the times of the Pharaohs in ancient Egypt. Whenever you want to protect yourself against anyone's bad intentions, wash your hands with this special cake of soap. Leave it to dry, then wrap it up in some bandages to protect the magic. Unwrap the soap whenever you need it again.

Wizardly spell tip: Carry a piece of turquoise with you as protection against evil.

Your Notes

Could you get all the ingredients?   *Yes* ☐ *No* ☐
_____

If not, list the other ingredients that you have used.
_____

_____

When did you do the spell?   *Time*   *Day*
_____

What Phase of the Moon is it?   *New Moon* ☐ *Waxing* ☐ *Full* ☐ *Waning* ☐

What happened during the spell? What thoughts occurred to you?
_____

_____

_____

_____

Did anything odd happen after the spell?
_____

_____

_____

_____

Do you think your spell worked?
_____

_____

Moon Magic Bathtub Spell

What Do I Need?
A bathtub
Bubble bath
A piece of white soap in the shape of a circle

When Do I Need to Do the Spell?
During the phase of the Full Moon, or any time you feel upset

What Should I Do?
This is a great spell to do if you are feeling very angry and unhappy. Sit in the warm bath and gaze at the Moon. If you can't see the Moon from your bathtub, pick up the circle of white soap and imagine that this is a piece of the Moon. When the Moon is full, it is believed to manifest its role as a kind and nurturing mother. Wash with the soap while imagining that all your cares are being soothed away, giving you space and ideas on how to handle your problems. When ready, let out the water, visualizing that all your anger and hurt is being taken away from you.

Your Notes

Could you get all the ingredients?   *Yes* ☐ *No* ☐

If not, list the other ingredients that you have used.

When did you do the spell?   *Time*   *Day*

What Phase of the Moon is it?   *New Moon* ☐ *Waxing* ☐ *Full* ☐ *Waning* ☐

What happened during the spell? What thoughts occurred to you?

Did anything odd happen after the spell?

Do you think your spell worked?

Garden of Dreams Spell

What Do I Need?

On a flat sheet or "dish" of steel, create a rock "garden" of the following stones:

> Tiger's eye
>
> Red jasper
>
> Hematite
>
> Citrine

Add to the stones, the following herbs:

> Lavender
>
> Chamomile

When Do I Need to Do the Spell?

Whenever you get nightmares

What Should I Do?

Construct the garden using the metal, stones, and herbs outlined above, and position the garden on your left-hand side as you are lying in bed. Just before going to bed, gaze at the garden, imagining that you are walking through it, feeling safe and well protected.

Your Notes

Could you get all the ingredients?   *Yes* ☐ *No* ☐

If not, list the other ingredients that you have used.

When did you do the spell?   *Time*   *Day*

What Phase of the Moon is it?   *New Moon* ☐ *Waxing* ☐ *Full* ☐ *Waning* ☐

What happened during the spell? What thoughts occurred to you?

Did anything odd happen after the spell?

Do you think your spell worked?

Wizard's Balm for Broken Hearts

What Do I Need?
A pot of glue and a brush
Some rose petals
A piece of rose quartz (or any pink-colored stone)
A piece of red cardboard shaped like a heart
A piece of red fabric

When Do I Need to Do the Spell?
Whenever you feel your heart has been broken

What Should I Do?
Take the heart-shaped piece of cardboard and tear it in half, putting all the hurt and unhappiness you feel into the tearing of the cardboard. Mix a few rose petals into the glue, then use a brush to apply it and stick the two pieces of the heart together (either one on top of the other or along the tear). Once the two pieces are stuck together, wrap the heart with a piece of red fabric, adding the pink-colored stone. Put the package in the noonday sunlight for three days and you will feel a lot better!

Your Notes

Could you get all the ingredients?   *Yes* ☐   *No* ☐
_____

If not, list the other ingredients that you have used.
_____

_____

When did you do the spell?   *Time*   *Day*
_____

What Phase of the Moon is it?   *New Moon* ☐ *Waxing* ☐ *Full* ☐ *Waning* ☐

What happened during the spell? What thoughts occurred to you?
_____

_____

_____

_____

Did anything odd happen after the spell?
_____

_____

_____

_____

Do you think your spell worked?
_____

_____

Your Notes

Your Notes

Your Notes

_____

_____

_____

_____

_____

_____

_____

_____

_____

_____

_____

_____

_____

_____

_____

_____

_____

_____

_____

_____

Your Notes

This edition published by Barnes & Noble, Inc.,
by arrangement with Lansdowne Publishing

2002 Barnes & Noble Books

ISBN 0-7607-3237-X

M 10 9 8 7 6 5 4 3 2 1

Commissioned by Deborah Nixon
Production Manager: Jane Kirby
Text: Anton and Mina Adams
Illustrator: Sue Ninham
Designer: Avril Makula
Editor: Patricia Dacey
Project Coordinator: Rea Hatzi-Fatouros

Set in Memento and Fontesque on Quark XPress
Printed in Singapore by Tien Wah Press (Pte) Ltd